LISTOGRAPHY, THE BOOK, IS DESIGNED TO HELP
YOU CREATE YOUR AUTOBIOGRAPHY THROUGH
LIST MAKING. I CREATED LISTOGRAPHY BECAUSE
I AM NOSTALGIC. I LOVE THE LITTLE DETAILS
OF LIFE, FROM EXPERIENCES TO FAVORITES, AND
I WANTED TO CREATE TWO NICE PLACES TO
CAPTURE AND SHARE THOSE DETAILS:
LISTOGRAPHY, THE BOOK, AND LISTOGRAPHY.COM.
I BELIEVE EVERYONE SHOULD HAVE AN
AUTOBIOGRAPHY, IF ONLY FOR THEIR LOVED
ONES TO READ AND EVEN IN THE SIMPLEST
FORM: A LIST.

LISA NOLA
WWW. LISTOGRAPHY. COM

Steve → I hope you enjoy this
I love you with every fiber of my
being! Merry Christmas 2014
Our first Christmas w/us & Moose & Brylan
& many more to come! Enjoy

LISTOGRAPHY

YOUR LIFE IN LISTS

CREATED BY LISA NOLA
ILLUSTRATED BY NATHANIEL RUSSELL

WWW. LISTOGRAPHY. COM

CHRONICLE BOOKS
SAN FRANCISCO

R.I.P.
FRANKIE
(1982 - 1982)

LIST PETS YOU'VE HAD
AND THEIR NAMES

Dogs: Sam   yellow lab mutt, Max black lab mutt
Shadrick AKA M2 black lab mutt still alive

- -

Cats: All cats are short hair unless otherwish
noted Oreo (had a few of these)
Scott, Tigger, Charlie, Foster
Senior year in H.S. got my gf. a kitten
her name was Misty she fell 5 stories
and broke her right leg in 2 places and
became the 3 leged wonder. Same time i got
misty back i obtained Rosco orange
tabby cat Misty ran away then i got
Esmerelda then Rosco ran away
↑ She is still here today
Had a few gold fish Frank was one of them
gerbal named Fritz and a hampster
Michale the turtle, frogs toads salamunders
and i believe thats it

Jan 12th
2015
7:45 pm

- -

- -

STEVEN

LIST MEMORABLE PEOPLE YOU'VE
WORKED WITH

Goodness I've worked at so many places i dont
even know where to start April 28th 10:30 Steve O. at McD
David at O'Mala's

ATTIC,
1492
VINE ST.

LIST PLACES YOU'VE LIVED

SMOKEY AND THE BANDIT II

SMOKEY IS THE BANDIT!

LIST YOUR FAVORITE FILMS

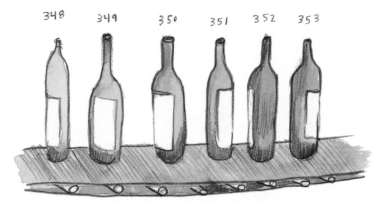

348   349   350   351   352   353

BOTTLE COUNTER
SUMMER OF 1992

LIST YOUR PAST JOBS

ALLIUMPHOBIA:
FEAR OF GARLIC

LIST YOUR BIGGEST FEARS

ON TOP OF REFRIGERATOR

LIST THE STRANGEST PLACES YOU'VE HAD SEX

I AM RELATED TO GANDHI

LIST THINGS MOST PEOPLE
PROBABLY DON'T KNOW ABOUT YOU

GRANDMA

LIST THE PEOPLE YOU LOVE THE MOST

LIST YOUR FAVORITE RESTAURANTS

LIECHTENSTEIN

LIST THE COUNTRIES YOU'VE VISITED

STICK

LIST YOUR FAVORITE TOYS YOU PLAYED WITH AS A CHILD

BEN, ASPIRING BASS PLAYER

LIST PEOPLE YOU'VE LIVED WITH

LIST YOUR FAVORITE BOOKS

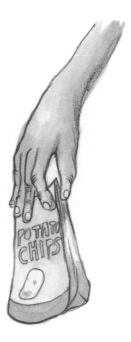

FIVE FINGER DISCOUNT

LIST YOUR BIGGEST SINS

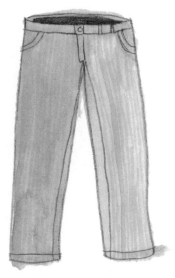

MOST COMFORTABLE PANTS EVER:
$3.95 AT THRIFT TOWN, 1994

LIST YOUR BEST PURCHASES

NANCY

LIST YOUR PAST LOVERS

LACK OF CONSIDERATION FOR OTHERS

LIST THINGS YOU'D LIKE TO CHANGE
ABOUT THE WORLD

KOJAK!

LIST YOUR FAVORITE TV
SHOWS OF ALL TIME

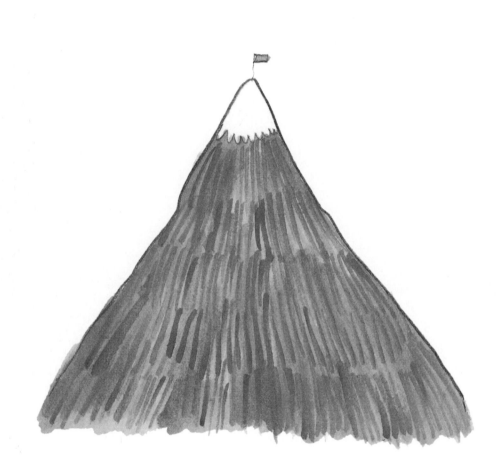

MT, CHIMICHANGA, CLIMBED IN 1987

LIST YOUR PROUD ACCOMPLISHMENTS

LIST YOUR FAVORITE BANDS

SUNDAY NIGHTS:

HOT FUDGE SUNDAE AND ROMANTIC COMEDY

LIST YOUR GUILTY PLEASURES

IRONIC MUSTACHES

LIST YOUR BIGGEST PET PEEVES

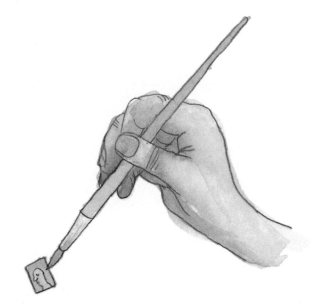

MINIATURE PORTRAIT PAINTING

LIST THE THINGS YOU'RE GLAD YOU DID

FAVORITE CHAIR

LIST THE THINGS YOU'D SAVE IF
YOUR HOME WAS ON FIRE

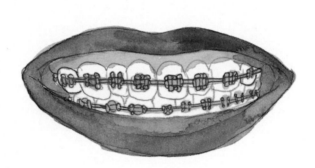

GOT MY BRACES OFF

LIST THE WAYS YOU'VE CHANGED SINCE YOUR TEENS

ABE   LINCOLN

LIST THE PEOPLE FROM
HISTORY YOU'D LIKE TO
HAVE A CONVERSATION WITH

THE ADVENTURES OF

GARFIELD

LIST YOUR FAVORITE ANIMATED MOVIES AND TV SHOWS

I STOLE YARD GNOMES THE
SUMMER OF 1990

LIST BAD THINGS YOU DID AS A KID

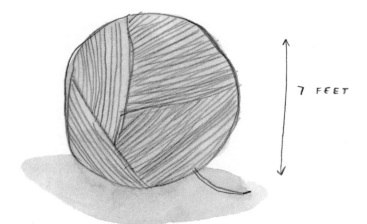

7 FEET

VISITED THE WORLD'S SECOND-LARGEST
BALL OF TWINE

LIST FUN THINGS YOU'VE DONE
IN YOUR TOWN

EXTREME KICKBALL

LIST YOUR FAVORITE GAMES TO PLAY

MADONNA "MATERIAL GIRL"

LIST YOUR FAVORITE SONGS

MY INCREDIBLY FIRM HANDSHAKE

LIST THE THINGS PEOPLE SHOULD
REMEMBER YOU FOR

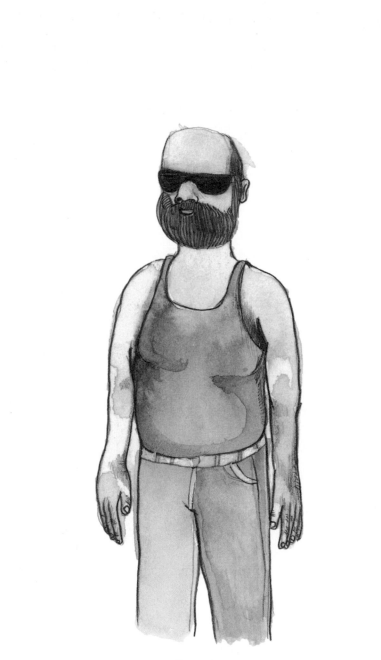

ROBERT

LIST THE MOST MEMORABLE

FRIENDS FROM YOUR PAST

YACHTING IN LUXURY

LIST THINGS YOU'D DO IF YOU WON THE LOTTERY

ATTENDED ANIMAL RIGHTS RALLY

LIST YOUR BIGGEST ACTS OF KINDNESS

GIRL AT THE DRUG STORE

LIST YOUR CRUSHES

DRUNKSQUIRREL.COM

LIST YOUR FAVORITE WEBSITES

.

LIST YOUR FAVORITE MAGAZINES

MRS. PHILLIPS
6TH GRADE EARTH SCIENCE

LIST YOUR FAVORITE TEACHERS

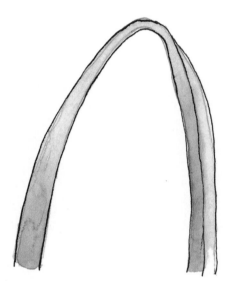

BEAUTIFUL DOWNTOWN ST. LOUIS

LIST THE AMERICAN CITIES YOU'VE VISITED

DEVO!

LIST BANDS YOU'VE SEEN LIVE

HOMECOMING

LIST THE TIMES YOU'VE
HAD AN AUDIENCE

MY FIRST PONY

LIST THE BEST GIFTS YOU'VE
EVER RECEIVED

ON THE MERRY-GO-ROUND

LIST YOUR MEMORABLE INJURIES
AND ILLNESSES

AL PACINO AS "SERPICO"

LIST YOUR FAVORITE MOVIE STARS

PEG-ROLLED
JEANS →

↑
MULTIPLE
SWATCHES

LIST YOUR PERSONAL FASHION
TRENDS OVER THE YEARS

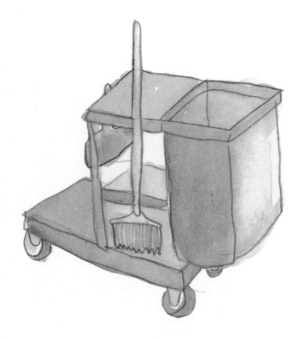

JANITORIAL SERVICE

LIST PROFESSIONS YOU'D LIKE TO TRY

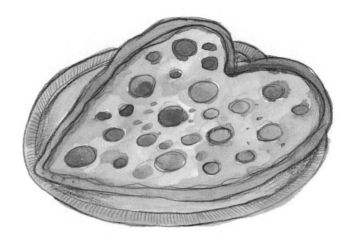

TENDENCY TO MAKE EVERYTHING
INTO HEART SHAPES

LIST THE THINGS YOU'D LIKE TO CHANGE ABOUT YOURSELF

LEGENDARY PABST BEER FACTORY

LIST THE PLACES YOU'D LIKE TO VISIT

REMAKE MY POPSICLE STICK TAJ MAHAL

LIST THINGS YOU WISH YOU HAD A SECOND CHANCE TO DO

WORK ON MY DJ SKILLS

LIST THE THINGS YOU LIKE
TO DO ON YOUR DAY OFF

CHRISTIE'S PARENTS'
HOT TUB

LIST ALL YOUR PAST HANG-OUTS

MY GARDENING SKILLS

LIST THE BEST THINGS ABOUT YOU

LIST YOUR MOST MEMORABLE

BIRTHDAYS OR HOLIDAYS

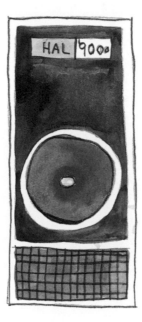

2001: A SPACE ODYSSEY SOUNDTRACK

LIST YOUR FAVORITE RECORDS

LIST THE NAMES OF PAST SCHOOLS
OR
CLASSES YOU'VE ATTENDED

I SAW ACE FREHLEY
AT THE AIRPORT

LIST FAMOUS PEOPLE YOU'VE ENCOUNTERED

HAWAIIAN LUAU, 1995

LIST THE MEMORABLE PARTIES
YOU'VE ATTENDED

LEARNED TO SURF

LIST YOUR GREATEST OUTDOOR ADVENTURES

CUTE KITTENS

CORN ON THE COB

LIST THINGS YOU
LOVE AND DESPISE

LIST CLUBS AND BARS
YOU'VE FREQUENTED

STAR WARS ACTION FIGURE COLLECTING

LIST YOUR HOBBIES PAST AND PRESENT

COMPULSIVE NOSE PICKING

LIST YOUR MOST EMBARRASSING
MOMENTS OR HABITS

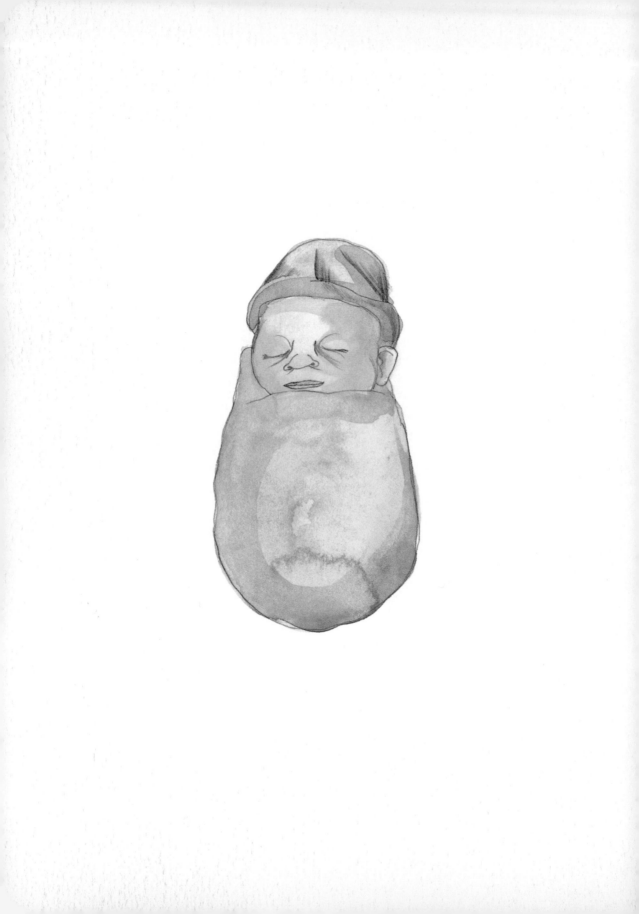

LIST THE BEST DAYS OF YOUR LIFE

_____

_____

_____

_____

_____

_____

_____

_____

_____

_____

_____

_____

_____

_____

_____

_____

_____

TAKE AN ART HISTORY CLASS

LIST YOUR LIFE "TO DO" LIST

MY STEPBROTHER'S
CHEAP WHISKEY

PONTIAC SUNBIRD HATCHBACK

SOUTHERN BAPTIST

FIRSTS

FIRST CAR

FIRST KISS

FIRST DRUG

FIRST RELIGION

FIRST

FIRST

FIRST

FIRSTS

FIRST

FIRST

FIRST

FIRST

FIRST

FIRST

FIRST

FIRSTS

FIRST

FIRST

FIRST

FIRST

FIRST

FIRST

FIRST

THONG, LAST MONDAY

DEAR JIMMY,
THINGS JUST
ARE'INT WORKING
OUT SO GOOD.
I'M OUT.
LOVE,
JULIE

A YEAR AND A HALF AGO

SEPTEMBER 2004

LASTS

LAST BIKE RIDE

LAST BREAK UP

LAST TIME I STAYED UP ALL NIGHT

LAST THING I LOST

LAST

LAST

LAST

LASTS

LAST

LAST

LAST

LAST

LAST

LAST

LAST

LASTS

LAST

- -

LAST

- -

LAST

- -

LAST

- -

LAST

- -

LAST

- -

LAST

- -

LISA NOLA EXPANDS HER LISTS INTO OTHER
FORMS OF WRITING IN HER SPARE TIME. SHE
EXISTS QUIETLY WITH HER PARTNER, HER
CATS, AND LISTOGRAPHY.COM. SHE IS FUELED
BY HER PROPENSITY FOR REFLECTION, HER
LOVE OF ORGANIZATION, AND TAKE-OUT FOOD.

PAST JOBS

SCHOOLTEACHER

PHOTOGRAPHER

WRITER

PIZZA MAKER

NIGHTCLUB OWNER

NATHANIEL RUSSELL WAS BORN, RAISED, AND EDUCATED IN INDIANA. HE NOW LIVES IN OAKLAND, CALIFORNIA, AND PASSES THE TIME DRAWING, READING, PLAYING MUSIC, AND DRINKING COFFEE. HE LOOKS FORWARD TO ONE DAY HAVING A HOUSE IN THE WOODS AND A CAT ON THE COUCH.

PAST JOBS

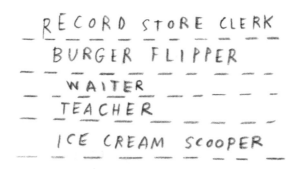

RECORD STORE CLERK
BURGER FLIPPER
WAITER
TEACHER
ICE CREAM SCOOPER

Design by Suzanne LaGasa
Illustrations by Nathaniel Russell
Manufactured in China
Chronicle Books endeavors to use environmentally
responsible paper in its gift and stationery products.

20 19 18 17 16 15 14 13

Chronicle Books LLC
680 Second Street
San Francisco, CA 94107
www.chroniclebooks.com